BLACKLIGHT

POETRY

Book 1:

GHETTO POETRY

BYRD THE OVERCOMER

Ghetto Poetry

The words "Ghetto" and "Poetry are two words that normally don't go together. When it comes to my life and times though, it seems the two words can't survive without the other one. There has always been a form of duality to my life. Maybe due to the fact that I had an obsession with comic books and proving myself worthy to just be. My two favorite DC comic's characters were, of course, Superman and Batman. Both troubled characters who had to live double lives in order to survive their environment. I would grow to admire Batman more because of his will and determination to make a difference no matter the cost. As a member of the Justice League he would become the most feared member, in spite of the fact he was the only regular person on the team. So, he always feels he has to prove himself even though he's the most dangerous.

I am not a product of the Ghetto. I've never been a street dude, a D-Boy, gangsta', member of anyone's gang. This is not the reason I title this book "Ghetto Poetry."The word Ghetto has a different meaning to different people. For me, it means hard, the obstacles that you have faced and conquered, the lack thereof or, the lack of resources, the realness of life, and the rawness of life. These are just a few definitions of what Ghetto means to me. I grew up around it. My words were ingrained by it. My morals and principles of life were definitely influenced by it. Blacklight Poetry and Ghetto Poetry are so very similar. They both represent the realness and the pressures of everyday life. There was a movie once that said, "We are not cute characters in poems." I have to disagree. I am one of many characters in my poems and stories.

This book is dedicated to all the voices that were never heard or taken seriously. The voices that were extinguished early by people that looked like them. The voices that were silenced by people who were appointed to protect and serve, yet, failed to do that job. The voices of those that never got to utilize their God Given Talent. The world has never been pretty and this country has never been truly great. However, your gift is beautiful and it is what's truly great. This collection of poetry is dedicated to all the Soul Searchers and Overcomer's who are out there still fighting to make a difference in this world. This is also dedicated to those on the front lines of change, trying to make a difference through these tough and turbulent times. I hope you enjoy once again diving into the mind of The Overcomer.

Stay motivated.

Table of Contents

Creation of an Intro

Some of the most entertaining people I've ever seen, whether on TV or in person always came out to a dope ass introduction. From Michael Buffer in boxing, Howard Finkel in Wrestling, Muhammad Ali, Floyd Mayweather; their entrances and introductions were sometimes just as or more entertaining than the actual event. So one day while at Poetic JB's house, we decided to write introductions for ourselves. It really was something that I wanted to do so maybe I took it a little more seriously than the other Soul Searchers. Either way, this is what I came up with:

The Introduction

Excuse me ladies and gentlemen,

May I please have your attention?

It's that Blacklight Poet,

That defies all descriptions

It's that friendly neighborhood Soul Searcher,

That's beyond any comprehension

It's that Inner City Poet,

Whose style is hard as long division

It's that man and a half,

Half Christian, half Heathen,

It's that Super Bowl, playoffs,

The regular and the preseason

It's that hood tested,

It's that ghetto approved

It's that stone that the building refused,

That simply will not be moved

It's that old school new school,

Pop locking meets the Nay Nay

It's that brand new piece dropper,

Every Poetry Drop Tuesday

It's that number one stunner,

Blacklight Poetry's frontrunner

The Muskogee Soul Searcher's heavyweight

champion!

Byrd the Overcomer

New Approach
To an Old Dream

We've come a long way,

But a lot of people have forgotten

A lot of people are no longer disenfranchised,

A lot of people are no longer downtrodden

Frederick said, "No Struggle No Progress,"

But man we've had our share

We've tasted the American Dream,

and even sipped on the nightmare

We've touched the surface of civil rights,

Growing ever so close to being equal

I not only do this for my loved ones,

I also do this for my people

Because I possess the soul of Langston Hughes,

Who told me to hold fast to my dreams

I got the tunnel vision of Brother Malcolm,

Who said find your worth by any means?

I try to motivate like Booker T. Washington,

Who said, "If you want to lift yourself up, lift up

someone else, Success is not measured by a man's

position or wealth. He's measured by the obstacles

he has faced, obstacles in which he had to
overcome."
This is for the ones who stood and fought for us,
this is even for those who wanted to run.
This is for the Mothers who chose to build strong
children, Instead of having to repair broken men.
This is for those who fell over, and over again,
But had the heart and faith to come back again
Harriet Tubman said, "Every great dream begins
with a Dreamer."
Is your Dream still within you?
Pastor King showed us the power and presence,
Of what just One Dreamer can do!!
It's time to come together once again with Love,
Not with anger or clenched fist.
Jesus said, "When two or three are gathered in my
name, I am in the midst."
So gather your love, gather your hope,
Gather your dreams, gather your faith
We've sat long enough in the tabernacles,
our homes, and our Secret Place
A lot of the younger generation is lost,
With no one left to lead them

So, without the love, the wisdom,

and the hope of the generation before,

They're left devouring whatever the world feeds

them

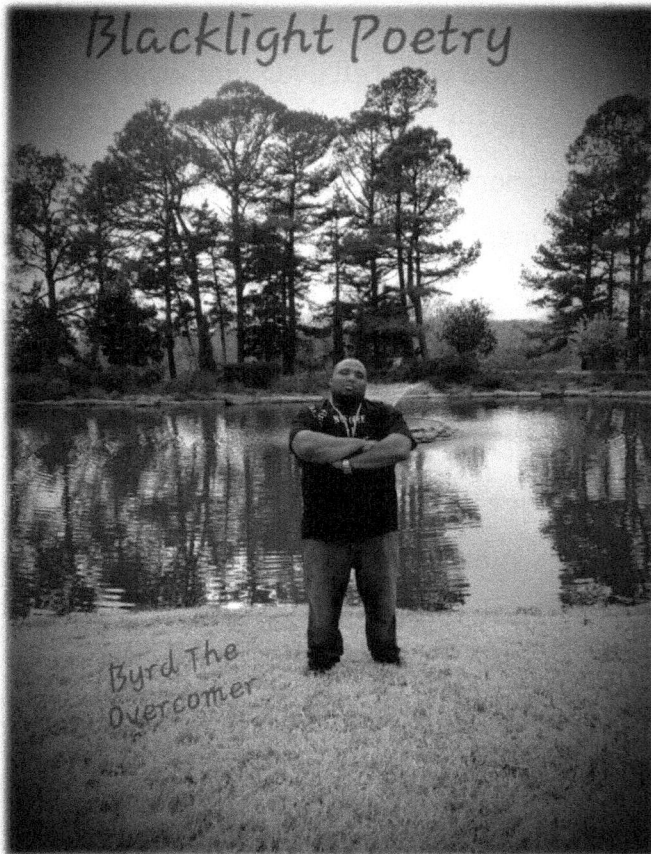

Perfectly Flawed

I'm perfectly flawed,

And that's okay.

I'll never be perfect but I'm faithful,

At the end of the day

I could never quit doing my thing,

Its part of the gift I was given

Stay motivated stay hungry,

Stay focused, stay driven

I've been delivered from those who judge,

They have no Heaven or Hell for me

I'm still standing in spite of the pits,

And the cells that they had planned for me I'm

trying to become the man,

That I was supposed to be

I'm still fighting everyday to unlock,

All the greatness in me

I'm still trying to see,

All the talent my Big Momma saw in me

All things considered, I haven't done badly

For a fat kid from Muskogee

But it's not near enough,

The surface has barely been scratched

I haven't caught half the stars,

That I have been ordained to catch

So I fly, keep flying,

With my cape still flapping

I'll let the entertainers entertain,

And let all the rappers keep rapping

Cause I'll always be judged by a different standard

That's ok I'm big enough to do it,

And hold up the banner

I'm Still Here

I'm walking through the valley of Death,

With Chuck Taylors and phat laces

Enemies are plotting my destruction,

With bad intentions and fake smiles on their faces

I hid for years in my sanctuaries,

Tabernacles and Secret Places

and praying for the day when I'd finally fly,

and be remembered as one of the greatest

So many obstacles slowed my journey,

My walk has been hit by setbacks

Taken so far off the track,

I didn't know if I'd ever find my way back

My walk was also slowed by self pity,

Lack of support from my city

Not knowing who was riding for me,

With me or against me

But I'm here still here,

Standing like Overcomer's do

Shining bright,

Not looking like what I've been through

Superman stature,

Walking like a King walk

Coming out my wilderness,

No longer a prisoner of my own thoughts

I'm allergic to being broke,

And I'm a fugitive from poverty

My soul is still intact,

It's under the protection of God's property

Lord I thank you,

Thank God I'm blessed

I was built to be an Overcomer,

So that's what I came to expect

Stay motivated.

Motivated

I got a quarter in my pocket,
Working towards a million
I let the haters have the room,
I'd rather buy the whole building
I never been the best,
But I'm always in the conversation
Walking in my purpose trying to,
Yield not into temptation
People are selling they soul,
For more followers on Twitter,
Hollering, "We should stick together,"
But the message never gets delivered
Amongst the broken glass,
Lies, the answers and solutions
To grow, you have to be able to get cut,
In spite of weak constitutions
In spite of fear and frustration,
In spite of trials and tribulations
In spite of bad circumstances,
and uncompromising situations
The power of life and death,
Resides in the tongue
I'm gonna' keep on pushing,
Until my Kingdom Come

Supreme

I had to have supreme hustle,

Mixed with just a little dash of Hood Muscle

I had my share of setbacks,

I had to fight through some struggles

I learned more from hitting rock bottom,

than I did reaching the mountain top

I promised Big Momma I'd toot my own horn,

I promised James I'd never stop

I promised Kou I'd keep it real,

I promised Blue I'd keep it true

I promised Boogi I'd show him to keep going,

Until the task is through

My vision is endless,

But the clock is ticking

I got to keep moving forward always,

To make my own happy ending

I lived long enough,

To watch my babies graduate

I take great pleasure,

in watching them all elevate

Someone has to be the baddest,

We are not all created equal

You can't fix broken people,

But broken people can break fixed people

Loyalty is a must,

Never abandon your team

Don't strive to be the best,

Strive to be SUPREME

Overcomer's Only Stand

Setback after Setback,

Overcomer's only stand

Big Momma Rowland told me there would be days,

When it'd be hard to stand up like a man

She also told me there would be days,

When things wouldn't all go according to plan

Setback after Setback,

Overcomer's only stand

Momma told me there would be days,

When it'd be hard for me to smile

I had to learn how to act grown,

Even when I was a child

I saw life consume friends,

People I loved dearly

To the point where it was hard,

To have or let anyone near me

I lost so many loved ones,

I lost so much ground

The sweet melodies of Christopher Wallace,

Was sometimes the only comforting sound

James told me Cape or no Cape,

I must fly like I'm Superman
Setback after Setback,
Overcomer's only stand

Dad taught me life is a Dog Fight,
and don't ever quit
Get your ass off of the couch,
If you ever plan to be rich
Practice don't make perfect,
Perfect practice makes perfect
Always bet the house on yourself,
Cause your dream is always worth it
Don't let anything stop your dream,
Not even you
Keep on catching the flames,
Nothing can stop you but you
There will always be pitfalls and obstacles
you face,
That you'll never understand
Setback after Setback,
Overcomer's only stand

Applause

I don't need any applause,

You don't have to clap for me

I am a Son of the Mic,

Just taking advantage of an opportunity

You see I've never been popular,

Never been anybody's favorite

As a matter of fact, most people I loved,

Told me that I would never make it

I shared my dreams with them,

And they shot them all down like Duck Hunt

That's why my drive is unexplainable,

Being good will simply never be enough

I cannot rest until every single ounce,

Of God Given Talent is completely spent

Until I have nothing else to write,

and God himself extinguishes my Blacklight

When I get to the gates,

I want to be completely empty

When God sees me I want to confidently tell him,

I used every ounce of talent you decided to give me

I shook the earth,

Just like you told me to do

Touched the lives of millions before I was through

As the gates swing open,

I see my Big Momma Rowland & Carter steady
clapping,

And James with his Superman Cape on,

Waiting to tell me everything that's happened

Kou throwing up a peace sign,

Hollering you're late

Jed wearing a huge smile,

Walking towards me holding my hot plate

Gary standing with his arms folded,

With Steelers tattooed on his angel wings

Kal'el and Storm run toward me waving,

Cause they've been misbehaving

See I don't need any applause,

Cause' I'll always have an audience I know that
claps for me

That's just how it is,

That's how it always is suppose to be

STAY MOTIVATED

During the dark times,

when you hear no applause and no one is calling your name,

Is when you need to take stock of what you really have

The relationships you've made

The mistakes you've made and paid for

The Comebacks, yes those Rocky Balboa moments

There were many times that quitting was a viable option

During those times, you really have to stay motivated

Think about those people that look up to you, some of whom you've never met

Your walk inspires others,

you'll never know how many

Cherish your God Given Talent

Use it, because it was given to you for a reason

I truly believe that if you don't adequately use your gift,

you will lose your gift

The worst thing in my city where I'm from is
wasted talent
Don't waste your talent
And above all else, stay motivated
No matter what
Even when the storms rage,
when your strength betrays you,
when your friends leave you,
and when it seems that hope has abandoned you
Stay motivated
Even when your own thoughts turn against you,
and you believe you're not worthy of your position
When you allow your fear to creep in, and you allow
it to infect your confidence
In those times remember this:

WHAT DOESN'T BREAK A MAN
MAKES A MAN

Stay motivated, you're not waiting for the miracle.
You don't have to
Because you are the miracle
Stay motivated

One Mic

All I need is one Mic, one piece,

One venue, and One stage

All I need is my Heart, my Lyrics,

Spilled onto a fresh blank page

A bottle of Ozark water,

Chilled perfectly to room temperature

I don't drop poetry,

I spit this Ghetto Scripture

I never been mainstream or accepted,

Or considered a role model

Never had much direction,

Or a certain pattern to follow

All I ever needed was one Mic,

One piece one team

A combination of million dollar lyrics

Mixed with one dream, one vision

I want to be remembered as a Wordsmith,

A poet filled with glorious purpose

To have the ability to bring relief,

To all those hurting

I always wanted to motivate the masses,

While at the same time motivating myself
To use my words to shake the earth,
To make my presence felt
I want to be the best at what I do,
And make some pennies from my pain.
Crawl out from under my family's shadow,
and finally establish a name
All I need is one Mic

Souls for Sale

I can't shoot a basketball,

Nor can I throw a baseball far

It's not worth selling my soul for a house,

clothes, or a badass car

They gave us the keys to a damaged vessel,

that they know for a fact it's already sinking

They dangle the carrot in front of the Mule

knowing,

Most will move forward absent of thinking

With words comes power,

But with power also comes frustration.

With frustration comes ignorance,

That eventually suffocates communication if a man

has the power to stop a riot,

Armed only with the bass of his voice

He has the obligation to speak,

I'm sorry he doesn't have much choice

The world needs those to kneel or stand up

This time, touchdowns won't ease the hurt

We got thousands dying from an invisible killer,

and got millions out of work

It's time to put work behind your Faith,

It's time to show why your Black Life Matters

You got the world's attention,

Now where's the peace you sought after?

This is our slim chance to change things,

In the little time we have

We have to come together off camera,

And rectify all the animosity we have

I don't know why it takes severe tragedy,

To bring us together

It makes us look so weak minded,

As if our cause is fair weathered

Give until it hurts,

then give until it stops hurting

Even if we lose this endeavor,

We must strive to keep moving, keep moving

A Talk with Myself

Byrd:

Hey Doyle, "what's up Boss?"
You sound a lot like you Hella defeated
Even when you took losses before,
You stood tall and you never retreated.
The things you can do with a paper and pen,
Man it astonishes most men
Okay, the pity party is over,
It's time to get back on track again

Doyle:

I don't know Boss,
Sometimes this weight is way too heavy to carry
I keep on trying to get ahead,
But it's like my situations and circumstances won't
let me
I never even asked for Love,
I just wanted the world to respect me
But sometimes I feel very alone,
Like the world is destined always to reject me

I have to work thrice as hard,

Just too barely make ends meet

You don't understand my frustration,

Nor do you feel my defeat

Byrd:

Wait, I don't understand?

Man, I don't know what's with you!

Through every high and though every low,

I have rode every single wave with you

The Soul Searchers have been with you,

No matter when, no matter where

Hell, you and Ink created "The Sons of the Mic,"

Out of thin air!

It was you who gave people something to believe in,

some people you've never met

You've built something out of nothing

Through blood, tears, and sweat

Through rhymes and lyrics

So many people had lost they voice,

You the one that taught them how to hear it

Doyle:

It still doesn't make it easy,
As life gets harder
Swimming with the piranhas,
While in shark infested waters

Byrd:

Shark infested waters,
What kind of talk is that?
How many times have we fallen',
Only to get up and come roaring back?
How many times have we manufactured victory,
in spite of superior opposition?
How many times have we won the crowd,
in spite of superior competition?
We did it before,
And we will do it again
Cause Overcomer's only stand,
And they don't make pacts with mere men

Doyle:

Thanks Boss, I needed that,
The pity party is a wrap!
I'm back in the bricks,
And I'm back bridging the gap
I'm strong enough to hold up the bridge,
I'm back on track
My setbacks have once again,
Set the open stage for my comeback.
I am *Doyle Rowland Jr.* aka *Byrd the Overcomer*,
Never to be mimicked or duplicated
It's time to practice what I preach
take my advice, and stay motivated

Dear Father

Dear Heavenly Father,

It's little me again.

I'm not coming to you,

as a Democrat or Republican

I come to you as a son of a King,

with a target on my back because of my skin. I

come to you as a Poet with promise,

With a mix of hurt and greatness spilling from his

pen

I'm hurting, but standing,

beyond my understanding

I've been trying to be a good shepherd,

and uphold all of your commandments

but the evil we face,

It's beginning to be too great

Our Kings are still being slaughtered,

whether in silence or even on tape

I'm in my secret place,

but I'm still feeling the flames

I still hear their screams,

I still remember their names

I know I'm not a saint,

I'm just an ambitious sinner
You definitely built an Overcomer,
You built a Breadwinner
I was built in your image,
I was raised by a village
I've been in this game,
This life is not a scrimmage
So many problems we're facing,
With inadequate representation
They a virus and some killer hornets,
Shut down a whole nation
A lot of the leaders fell silent,
They closed the doors of the church
Millions of people are jobless,
Getting laid off work
I know that this is all,
Somehow part of your plan
It's not my job to question,
It's my job only to stand
I'm standing on your word,
I'm standing on your promise
I'm standing on my Faith that I lost,
Hey, I'm just being honest

I'll continue to stand,

I'm standing in the gap

I will keep using the gifts that were given,

Until you come and take this life back

My God our Father,

Please don't let the enemy take us under

Sincerely and eternally yours,

Byrd the Overcomer

Byrd Insider

This love of writing had very crazy beginnings. My love for poetry actually started as a punishment. I went to school at Sadler Elementary, the real Sadler Elementary before it became a Science academy. Anyway, we had bad weather so we were inside for recess. Some friends and I occupied ourselves by shooting some dice in the corner. Hey, it's arithmetic right? Yeah, Mrs. Johnson, the teacher that caught us didn't think so either. She took the dice and the change that was on the floor. As punishment for this offense she made each of us sit down and write a poem about Martin Luther King Jr., since his holiday was coming up. All the other guys just blew it off, but I knew I couldn't cause my Mom was teaching right down the hall and she didn't play. So I wrote a little piece about the King and gave it to Mrs. Johnson. I didn't think it was that good, but she seemed to think it was good. She showed it to all the other teachers, including my Mom. They liked it so much they "voluntold" me to recite the piece at the Black History program the next week in front of the whole school. The piece itself didn't excite me. It was the reaction of everyone else. I loved writing stories more than I liked poetry, so I didn't write poetry again until I was in Junior High.

Blacknificent

I'm a descendant of Kings,

I'm a Son of the Mic

I'm patiently waiting for the Kingdom to come,

While standing under the Blacklight

Where my body may fail,

My words will prevail

I'm attempting to bridge all the gaps,

With knives still stuck in my back

I'm still standing big and tall,

Even after surviving Thanos' snap

The Covid couldn't silence me,

The Hornets couldn't sting me

I hid often in my Secret Place,

The enemy couldn't see me

If anything it freed me,

It gave me time to think

It gave me time to write,

A lifetime of experiences in Ink

Eventually becoming the best,

Has never been the intent

I spill Soul on these pages,

That makes me Blacknificent

After all the fame,

After the money's been spent

I will still stand erect,

I'll be Blacknificent

These words are not mine,

This here is God Given

I have yet to get my stuff back,

Until then I got to stay driven

My struggles made me a King,

My hunger made me a Beast

I stayed down long enough,

I was overdue for an increase

Overdue for a release

I recovered from my defeats

I never ever wanted it all,

I just simply wanted my piece

I had to invest,

To get my 20%

I got a Brand to protect,

and that's simply Blacknificent

I spill my Soul on these pages,

That makes me Blacknificent

After the fame is gone,

After the money has been spent

I will still stand erect,

I will still remain Blacknificent

A Million

Make no mistake,

I have been that Sooner State Heavyweight

I'm not always at my best,

But I guarantee everything I drop is great

I prayed and wrote my fate,

My blood is spilled on this piece of paper

I had to learn to keep it Hondo,

Amongst enemies and a sea of haters

Ink got me feeling Beautifully Savage,

While rhyming in bunches like I'm Aaron Sawyer

Like Honey B my flow's as sweet as the white stuff,

In my hands this pen becomes the sword of Conan the Destroyer

I'm a King, I'm a leader,

I wanna shake the world like King MAC and Queen Sharita

In the confines of Poetic City,

I want to build my own arena

I'm feeling so creative like I'm Bleek,

I'm trying to get you higher than Harvey's new
growth
I'll never claim to be the greatest,
but I'll claim that I want it the most
I got a little JB in me,
Cause right now I'm feeling like a Master
I am Byrd the Overcomer,
The wrong entity to try to come after

I got that Unicron Hunger,
I devour most of my opposition
I try not to let my not to let my emotions show,
Cause I have the capacity to knock whole factions
out of commission
Just like Keya I got Soul,
Sometimes it's hard for me to think
But I always keep it Smooth,
With a touch of Invisible Ink

My Flow is so Breezy never sleazy,
They try to catch me but they can't see me
I can't put the Mic down,
Until I conquer totally and completely

I've never made love to the Mic,
I've just never been that subtle
They have awakened the Byrdman again,
Ink should have never removed my muzzle

Poetry is my Passion,
I back down from no challenge
I bring it all to the table,
Topped with some God Given Talent
You asked for it you begged for it,
So that Blacklight Poet is here
This is a Million Dollar Piece,
I'm just waiting for the check to clear

Mac n Cheese

Oh my Damn Baby Girl,
Your body dial is set on Magnificent
I'm addicted to your Melanin,
You got me harder than police questioning
Those thighs are speaking a language,
Only a Soul Searcher can decipher
Your curves are a physical aphrodisiac,
Making and taking this situation higher

Baby, let's have our own versus battle,
You're Love Jones vs. my Love Stroke
Tip toe down highway 69,
And let's see who'll be the first to choke
WAP versus BAD,
Truly a clash of the Titans
The event of the Century,
Bring your pussycat, cause' tonight we are dog
fighting

It's time to show and tell,
No wolf tickets if you please.
I'd like an order of Honey Love,

With two sides of Mac n Cheese
Let me stir your Mac n Cheese,
Like Big Momma's wooden spoon
Star in the early morning,
And don't get done until late afternoon

Like a MMA fight,
Let me give you these five championship rounds
And let the neighbors beat on the walls,
Complaining about the sounds
If you have never heard of Mac n Cheese Love,
I can show you better than I can tell you
Let Byrd make you an Overcomer,
I promise I won't fail you

Giggle and Shake

They tell me real women giggle,

They also tell me real women shake

I don't shop for snacks,

Cause I love eating pound cake

I love my steak and potatoes,

When I can't have my grilled chicken salad

I love to see a woman with goals

Whose walking in their God Given Talent

I like my women like I like my pancakes,

Cause I know for a fact that Thick Thighs Matter

I love it when they Sweet like syrup,

And thick like batter

My full figured Queens,

This is for all of my BBWs

This is for all the scary guys from afar,

Who have been secretly, loving you

Worrying about opinion,

Worrying about reputation

When you have a sexiness that's unmatched

And possess incredible conversation

My Queens of the world,

I salute you

May your future King treat you like the Queen that
you are,
And never misuse you

One More Time

One more time,

I'm gonna stare straight into the abyss

One more time, I'm a withstand the heat,

Cause I was built for this shit

One more time,

I'm going to let them mispronounce my name

One more time until this thing is over,

Things will never again be the same

One more time I'm going to allow them to shower me,

With glass praises and fake love

One more time, I'll get close enough,

For my enemies to touch

One more time I'll confess I love you,

Cause my love has been proven

One more time, I'll wave goodbye,

Cause it's time to keep moving

One more time, one last time,

You're gone see my face.

One more time, one more defeat,

Before I finally catch up to my faith

The Defiant

My road has never been a straight one,

It's always filled with detours and slow traffic

I had to push and pull for every inch

Nothing for me was automatic

Writing has been my refuge,

Poetry is my Passion

I guarantee we're built different,

Cause I started above average

I looked at Heaven from a distance,

As I gingerly walked through Hell

I've paid the price to spit nice,

I lost count of every time that I fell

I lost count of every time that I came up short

Whether it was a bad diagnosis,

Or on the wrong end of divorce

Now I'm standing with promise,

After walking with purpose

I learned that I may not be perfect,

But I'm faithful and I'm worth it

Now the enemy's all nervous,

Because they have awakened a fire breathing giant
Now I'm standing for all the world to see
All Blacknificent and as "The Defiant"

Melanated

Let me first start by saying you're valued,
You don't look like what you've been through
You're looking, and smelling, and tasting,
Better than Big Momma's cooked food
Your curves are outrageous,
Your spirit is contagious.
From every direction I see perfection,
You're so fly that you're weightless

The way that you move can only be,
Described as Poetry in Motion
When you get them hips to switching,
It causes quite a commotion
We have fantastic conversation,
Baby you are the total package
All big, bad and bougie,
A Wonderfully and Fearfully made Savage

Oh my damn! Allow me to be your Superman,
You can be my Wonder Woman
This feeling is so unexpected,
I never saw any of this coming

I find myself addicted to your Brown Skin,
Your Melanin is my narcotic
All that ass defies logic,
At times to me you're so erotic

You're like a wave of pure ecstasy,
And it's impossible for me to stop it
Looking like you walked out of a comic,
Got me higher than the strongest chronic
You're always the center of attention,
Because the way you move is so melodic
You know you bad now stop it,
Whatever you tried to prove you topped it
I feel for the soul who did you dirty,
Cause you made sure he never forgot it

Let me finish by saying you're valued,
You don't look like what you've been
through
I see that crown on your braided brow,
Go ahead and go be the Queen that's in you

I Am

I am the Son of the Mic,
A Son of a God
I am a Blacklight Poet,
Who triumphs against all odds
I am always considered secondary,
Even though life has me feeling legendary
I am the voice of the voiceless,
That became necessary

I am a Father to many,
I am a husband of one
I am a product of Muskogee,
But I'm more than just where I am from
I am the storm no one expected,
The stone that the building rejected
My president is Green,
No matter who is elected

I am the stroke of the pen,
I am the sweet smell of the wind. I am the power
behind the praise,
I am the beginning, middle, and the end
I Am.

Be Your Ironman

Please allow me to be your Ironman,

I'll be your Toney Stark

Your body is shining like a Mark 5,

With more curves than a Question Mark

I wish I could just fly you out to an island

Where I can slowly love you past 3000

Baby I'm not a super soldier,

But for you I'd take on a battalion

I'd take on a whole squadron,

Because I know your love is worth it

This love between us may never make sense,

Because I know it's far from perfect

But here we both are,

Fighting for our life in this Endgame

Our love has never been built the same,

Ever since you took on my last name

Please allow me to be your Ironman,

And I'll need you to be my Pepper

I'm trying to love you past 3000,

Into infinity or until forever

Indeed

As they plotted my destruction,
My focus stayed as consistent as percussion
Being great has always been the destination,
Quitting has never been the subject of discussion
Everyone can quit tomorrow,
I'm sorry I've never had that luxury
Cause I'm leaning on his arms,
And he never stopped loving me

I'm not a fair weathered Christian,
I praise him no matter how I'm living
Through a premature birth,
And countless attacks
No matter how hard he lets me fall,
He's always my source of power in my comeback
Some say singing don't change things,
I say that's a bunch of bullshit

Cause sometimes that's the only form of weapons,
That is available to take up arms and fight with
Sometimes I only have the strength to raise my
hands and say Lord I thank you

Sometimes my faith ain't enough,

And I only have the strength to praise you

Sometimes prayer is all I have

And sometimes it's all that I need

All I know is that he's always on time,

And he's been good to me and mines indeed

Rocky

Put some respect on my name get it right,

I am Byrd the Overcomer

My rhyme style is Covid,

I shut down the whole summer

I'm a born again wordsmith,

Not many people can out write me

I'm kind feeling like Trump,

Cause there's a lot of niggas that don't like me

They think I'm something like my Brother's,

Maybe I'm just like my Father,

I'm just a Blacklight Gym General,

Half Sir, half Survivor

Yes the black MacGyver,

The way that I manufacture classics

I'm more Hulk than Hogan,

More Macho Man than Savage

I want it so bad cause' I wasn't born with it,

Then they fucked up and told me I'd never be

strong enough to get it.

Now your boy is screaming up at the Heavens,

"Big Momma your Lil Byrd did it!"
There's poetry in my pedigree,
Sprinkled with some God Given Talent
Most of the time I stay tamed,
Until I feel threatened or a challenge

Then that Beast comes knocking,
Snorting and spitting
Veins filled with ice,
Fully equipped for wig splitting
I'm Pac, I'm Guru, I'm Big L,
I'm Biggie
When I hit the stage and grab the Mic,
I carry all they spirits with me.

I was born for this shit,
Iceman couldn't come more colder
I took Superman's S,
And slapped the shit on my shoulder
Took his cape off,
And use it as a bandanna
Even Batman looked up and said,
Byrd you a bad Mamma Jamma!

Oh my dam someone stop me,
The Diabetes couldn't drop me
I'm a born Underdog,
The poetic equivalent of Rocky

Still a Nigga

No matter how much money I make,
No matter how many positive steps I take
No matter how many milestones I shatter,
No matter how many records I break
To them,
I'm still a Nigga

I can compose the sweetest of ballards,
I can write poetry that will make your soul rattle
I can be on the frontline of every war,
And be the victor I every single battle
But to them,
I'm still a Nigga

I could help change the world,
Go to church every Sunday
Be a great Father to my children,
I could make lots of legal money
Bring Crips and Bloods together,
Through my poetry bring about real change Treat
everyone with respect,
Bring honor to my name

But to them,

I'm still a Nigga.

Whether they know my name,

Or even read my words

No matter how fantastic I am,

At manipulating these nouns and verbs

No matter how talented,

No matter how fine,

No matter how many times I take the stage,

And make the microphone mine

No matter how many losses,

No matter how many victories I rack up

No matter how good I feel,

No matter how bad I'm jacked up

No matter how much this Soul Searcher changes
the world

No matter how good a man I become,

And do good in this world

To them,

I'm still a Nigga.

No Dream is too Big.

Follow your vision. Stay motivated.